Material Detectives: Water

Let's Look at a Puddle

Angela Royston

Heinemann Library
Chicago, Illinois

Printed and bound in China by South China Printing Company Limited
Photo research by Erica Newbery

10 09 08 07 06
10 9 8 7 6 5 4 3 2 1

Library of Congress Cataloging-in-Publication Data
Royston, Angela.
  Water : let's look at a puddle / Angela Royston.
      p. cm. -- (Material detectives)
  Includes index.
  ISBN 1-4034-7676-4 (lib. bdg.) -- ISBN 1-4034-7685-3 (pbk.)
 1. Water--Juvenile literature. I. Title. II. Series.
  QD169.W3R64 2005
  553.7--dc22

                                        2005004709

Acknowledgments
The author and publishers are grateful to the following for permission to reproduce copyright material: Alamy pp. **22** left, **24** top; Creatas pp. **20**, **23** (solid); David Muench/Corbis p. **10**; Getty Images/Photodisc pp. **19**, **23** (float); Ivan J Belcher/Worldwide Picture Library/Alamy pp. **22** right, **24** bottom; Lesley Pardoe/PBPA (Paul Beard Photo Library) p. **18**; National Geographic/Getty pp. **4**, **23** (dip); Photodisc p. **16**; Picture Plain/Photolibrary pp. **15**, **23** (disappear); Rebecca Emery/Corbis p. **5**; Sarah Chappelow pp. **21**, **23** (melts); Satushek Steve/Photolibrary p. **9**; Star/Zefa p. **14**; stock4b/Felbert + Eickenberg/zefa p. **13**; Tudor Photography/Harcourt Education Ltd pp. **6**, **7**, **8**, **11**, **12**, **17**, **23** (liquid).
Cover photograph of puddles reproduced with permission of Comstock Images/Getty Images.

Every effort has been made to contact copyright holders of any material reproduced in this book. Any omissions will be rectified in subsequent printings if notice is given to the publisher.

Many thanks to the teachers, library media specialists, reading instructors, and educational consultants who have helped develop the Read and Learn/Lee y aprende brand.

Some words are shown in bold, **like this**. They are explained in the glossary on page 23.

Contents

What is a Puddle?

A puddle is a small pool of water.

A puddle forms in a **dip** in the ground.

Some puddles are deeper than
other puddles.

What is Water?

Water is a **liquid**.

Liquids are wet and runny.

water

milk

banana

cookie

Which of these things are liquids?

Milk and water are **liquids**.

They are both wet and runny.

Water falls from the sky as rain.

It makes puddles on the ground.

What Shape are Puddles?

Puddles are many different shapes and sizes.

Water runs all over the place.

That means puddles can be any shape.

Can Puddles Change Size?

You can make a puddle bigger by pouring more water into it.

What happens to a puddle when the sun shines on it?

A puddle gets smaller when the sun shines on it.

The sun makes the water dry up.

If the sun shines for a long time, a puddle will **disappear**.

How Can You Make a Splash?

When you jump into a puddle, you make a big splash.

rock

brick

leaf

twig

If you threw these things into a big puddle, which ones would make a splash?

The rock and the brick would make splashes because they are heavy.

Some things **float** on water.

The leaf and the twig would float in the puddle.

When Does a Puddle Turn into Ice?

A puddle turns into ice when it gets very cold.

Ice is **solid** water.

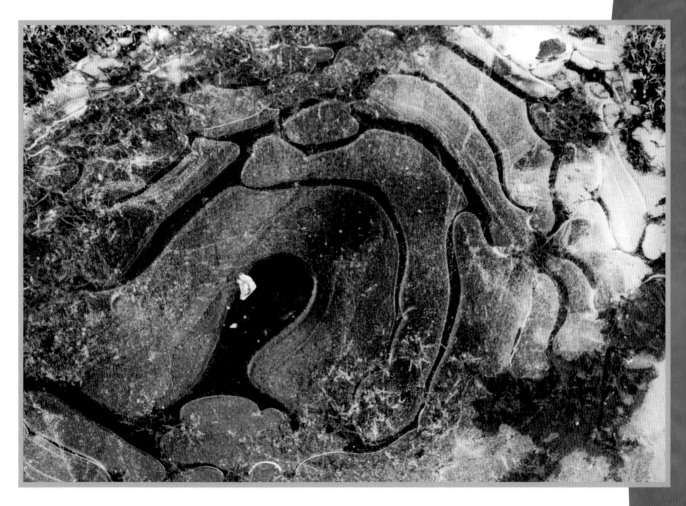

When the ice **melts**, it turns back into water.

Quiz

Which of these puddles will get bigger?

Which puddle will get smaller?

Look for the answers on page 24.

Glossary

dip
shallow hole or hollow

disappear
go away so that you cannot see it

float
not sink to the bottom

liquid
something wet you can pour

melts
becomes warmer and turns from a solid
into a liquid

solid
something that keeps its shape by itself

Index

Answers to quiz on page 22

The puddle in the rain is getting bigger because more water is falling into it.

The puddle in the sun will get smaller because the sun will dry up the water.

Note to parents and teachers

Reading for information is an important part of a child's literacy development. Learning begins with a question about something. Help children think of themselves as investigators and researchers by encouraging their questions about the world around them. Each chapter in this book begins with a question. Read the question together. Look at the pictures. Talk about what you think the answer might be. Then read the text to find out if your predictions were correct. Think of other questions you could ask about the topic, and discuss where you might find the answers. Assist children in using the picture glossary and the index to practice new vocabulary and research skills.